Jokes To Read
in the Dark

SCOTT CORBETT

Jokes To Read in the Dark

pictures by Annie Gusman

A TRUMPET CLUB SPECIAL EDITION

Published by The Trumpet Club
a division of Bantam Doubleday Dell Publishing Group, Inc.
666 Fifth Avenue, New York, New York 10103

ISBN: 0-440-84256-5

This edition published by arrangement with E. P. Dutton,
a division of Penguin Books USA Inc.
Editor: Emilie McLeod   Designer: Riki Levinson
Printed in the United States of America
October 1990

10 9 8 7 6 5 4 3 2
CW

for Stanley Summer

So You Want To Write Bad Jokes—
AN INTRODUCTION

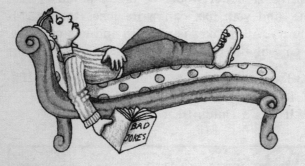

This book will do one of two things for you. Either it will teach you to write bad jokes, or prove you can't. And don't think learning how will be easy. Writing bad jokes is no laughing matter. If you read this book and still haven't learned anything, then take up bird-watching instead of bad joke writing. It's better for you anyway, because it gets you out into the fresh air. Most bad jokes are written in stuffy rooms.

The best way to write bad jokes is with a pencil, so that you can erase them. Jokes are hard to write, so use a hard lead pencil. Write them in a secret code if you can, and try to disguise your handwriting.

There are many types of BJs, but we will mention only a few here. One of the worst types of BJ is the "is-so" joke:

My little brother is so dumb he thinks an encyclopedia is something on three wheels.

Any BJ writer would be pretty proud of that one, and you, too, can write jokes that bad if you try. All it takes is practice and lots of nerve. One of the oldest BJs we have is the riddle:

Q. Two cannibals ate a missionary from Holland and split the dinner check. Why?
A. It was a Dutch treat.

Another common type of BJ is the knock-knock:

> Knock! knock!
> *Who's there?*
> Upton.
> *Upton who?*
> Upton no good.

Elephant jokes are also very big in the BJ field. What did elephants ever do to deserve these? Nobody tells hyena jokes, but hyenas laugh at elephant jokes and everything else.

Even elephant jokes and knock-knocks, however, are harmless compared to limericks. Where limericks are concerned, here's a word of warning:

If it's limericks you're longing to write, then you're in a deplorable plight; if you read them aloud to your neighborhood crowd, they'll all move away in the night. Once you're caught in the limerick's grip, it's worse than the plague or the pip; in writing, we're told, the limericks hold the featherweight championship.

And *never* read more than ten pages of BJs at one sitting, or even one standing. Think of your health!

A swami named Rami K. Dass
Who walked on his hands wished to pass
    Through a village at dawn,
    But he came to a lawn
With a sign that said, Hands Off the Grass!

Knock! knock!
Who's there?
Gwynne.
Gwynne who?
Gwynne the house and stay there!

HERE LIES
THE BODY
OF
WILFRED
WHITE

HIS BULLETPROOF
VEST WASN'T QUITE

I always try to avoid Stanley Winters, but yesterday he saw me coming first.

"What's the difference between a basketball player who skins his knee and a bunch of sand fleas?" he asked. I didn't know. He told me. "The basketball player makes a sports scar, but sand fleas make a beach buggy."

So now you know why I try to avoid Stanley Winters.

My Uncle Jasper is so bald
he makes a bowling ball look fuzzy.

———•———

Q. Two lions played poker for a giraffe. Why were they nervous?
A. They were playing for high steaks.

———•———

Cover-Up

The emblem on the shield
Of Sir Roger Littlefield
Was a moon of silvery white;
'Neath a cloak of sable hue
He hid it from view
Thus becoming a dark moonless knight.

———•———

A girl named Ruth Booth from Duluth
Who lisped very badly, forsooth,
    Said, "I'm glad I'm Ruth Booth
    And come from Duluth,
And not Thuthie Thmith from Thaint Looth!"

    Knock! knock!
    Who's there?
    Althea.
    Althea who?
    Althea in church Thunday.*

    Knock! knock!
    Who's there?
    Dewey.
    Dewey who?
    Dewey or don't we?'

A thankful young fellow named Fred
Said, "My favorite color is red.
    I'm one lucky fellow!
    It might have been yellow—
And I *hate* yellow!" That's what he said.

---

6   ** Two lisping jokes in a row! That's really bad!*

Just when I was enjoying myself at the zoo, Stanley Winters pounced on me.

"What are you doing out of your cage?" he asked.

"Now, listen, Stanley—"

"I hear the lion doesn't like his new cage. He preferred life in old den times."

"Stanley—"

"So did the lioness. She misses being a den mother."

"Stanley, will you—"

"Of course, it was their father who took the little cubs on stalking hikes and taught them to be cub scouts."

"Help!"

Our dog is so big he never bites postmen,
he swallows them whole.

———•———

Hard Luck Story

One very dark night on the heath
Count Dracula chipped his front teeth
    When he thought he espied
    His new-chosen bride
Out walking alone on the heath.

He confided to me with a groan,
What he saw in the dark as her own
    Lovely neck and a shoulder
    Was an oddly shaped boulder—
And you cannot get blood from a stone!*

———•———

    Double limericks are against the law in Timbuktu.

SIX-GUN
McGRAW

Here lies the body of Six-Gun McGraw;
His mother-in-law was quick on the draw.

It's Something, Y'know,
That I, Y'know, Don't Care For

When every other thing you say
    Is "Y'know," you never sell me;
My impulse is to say, y'know,
    "No, I *don't* know. Tell me!"

CONVERSATION ON ANOTHER PLANET

"Have a good vacation?"

"Not bad, but it's nice to be home among normal people."

"Where did you go?"

"Well, this time we tried Earth."

"Earth? Oh, yes. I've heard it's a nice little planet——but what about those creatures that live on it? Are they as weird as I've always heard they are?"

"Are they ever! You have to see them to believe them——freaks with just two arms, two legs, and only one head!"

Knock! knock!
Who's there?
P. S.
P. S.? I thought your name was Adeline.
Well, P. S. *is* when you Adeline.

Honesty Is the Best Policy

When George was but a boy, quite wee,
He chop-ped down a cherry tree.
His father found it chop-ped down,
And ask-ed Georgie with a frown,
"What is this thing that here I see?
Who chop-ped down this cherry tree?"
Said George, "I cannot tell a lie.
I do not care for cherry pie."
Then said his pa with gladsome cry,
"To tell the truth, son, neither do I!"

Knock! knock!
Who's there?
That's my knees! I'm scared!

My grandpa was so strong he could pitch horse-
    shoes
without taking them off the horse.*

---

* These are sometimes called was-so jokes.

Beale's Last Ride

There once was a man named Beale,
Whose nerves were made of steel;
    He went for a drive
    With a Thing not alive—
With a Creature, quite dead, at the wheel.

Now, a bit absentminded was Beale,
Who at first didn't notice, or feel
    There was anything wrong,
    But then, before long,
The driver, he saw, seemed to reel.

"Just what is your trouble?" asked Beale.
"Please stay on an evener keel!"
    As they went off a cliff
    He said to the stiff,
"Pull over! I'm taking the wheel!"

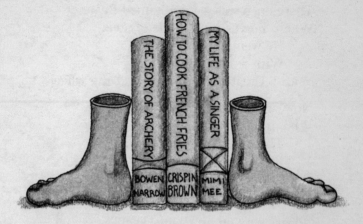

THE STORY OF ARCHERY — BOWEN NARROW

HOW TO COOK FRENCH FRIES — CRISPIN BROWN

MY LIFE AS A SINGER — MIMI MEE

I'll never forget the day our state started charging sales tax on everything, because that was the day Stanley Winters caught me in a rug store.

"Don't buy any more rugs!" said Stanley. "Who wants to get stuck with a lot of carpet tax? I feel sorry for the rug dealers, they're really floored, and their product takes a beating. Personally, I'd rather be a tuba manufacturer, nobody's going to take the wind out of his sales!"

"Stanley, you try my patience!"

"No, you try mine, I've got more of it."

Winter Bulletin

The nudists left their camp today.
The sign on the fence says Clothed Till May.

Growing Boy

Sometimes the size of the meals
    I eat at night
Are enough to make me lose
    My appetite.

Q. Why does an elephant want to be alone?
A. Because two's a crowd.

THOMAS
STROMM

Here lies the body of Thomas Stromm,
The inventor, he thought, of a foolproof bomb.

OLD JOKES NEVER DIE

"I entered a long distance spitting contest and
only took third place."
"Well, how did you expect to rate?"

SHOOT-OUT AT HIGH NOON

The wide main street of the dusty cow town was empty at high noon except for one grim figure at each end of the sunbaked street.

Slowly the two gunmen began to walk toward each other. When they were no more than ten feet apart, they stopped.

"Howdy, Tex. Who you lookin' fer?"

"Sidewinder Jenkins. Who you lookin' fer, Bat?"

"The Coyote Kid."

"Well, it don't look like neither of them yellow-bellies is gonna show up, so let's get in outa the hot sun," said Tex, and they headed for the Last Chance Saloon.

Thanksgiving Day

Upon a certain Thursday
 Every turkey cowers.
They observe Thanksgiving Day
 On the Friday after ours!

Q. Which restaurants do the best business during Lent?

A. Fast food chains.

My sister Louise is so pale
she makes a ghost look sunburned.

Knock! knock!
Who's there?
Hyman.
Hyman who?
Hyman old cowhand.

JOSEPH STOWE

Here lies the body of Joseph Stowe,
Better known as "Grand Canyon Joe."
Walked on a ledge. Stubbed his toe.
After that . . . only one way to go.

NEW BOOKS

THE FLOATING ZOO
BY NOAH ZARK

WELL, I NEVER!
BY IDA CLARE

THE EARRING LOVER
BY PIERCE STEERS

There was a young lady from Maine
Who gave everybody a pain,
 Though what was the cause
 (Except for her claws)
I never could quite ascertain.

———•———

Knock! knock!
Who's there?
Sawyer.
Sawyer who?
Sawyer picture in the paper.

THE COWARDLY ARCHER
A Tale of the Middle Ages

McNiver was a yeoman bowman
Who always feared to face the foeman;
They always saw McNiver quiver,
And also saw his quiver quiver;
McNiver had a lily liver,
McNiver never failed to shiver,
He never stood his ground, McNiver,
Of ground he ever was a giver,
He gave it up to any foeman,
McNiver did, that yeoman bowman,
That next-to-no-man totem-low-man,
That anything but go-go-go-man!

NEW BOOK

How To Take A Census
by Harmony Arthur

SHIRLEY
SCHIFF

Here lies the body of Shirley Schiff;
Chased a Frisbee off a cliff.

THE MOTHS AND THE MISER'S PURSE

Once upon a time two moths were sitting in a miser's purse.

"Why were we put here?" grumbled one moth. "We can't eat gold or silver. This is ridiculous!"

"You don't understand," said the other. "When the miser opens his purse we'll fly out, and that's supposed to show how stingy he is."

"In other words, the whole thing is just a big joke!"

Just then the miser picked up his purse, but instead of opening it he put it in his pocket and took it with him to the next town twenty miles away.

Moral: Some people carry a joke pretty far.

FENIMORE
FLEET

Here lies the body of Fenimore Fleet;
Looked one way on a two-way street.

THE POOR OLD OWL

Once upon a time there was an old owl who
lived in a drafty hollow tree.

One day he pulled on a pair of warm socks.
One sock had a hole in it, so he caught a darn-
ing needle to mend it with, but before he could
finish he had also caught a cold. His eyes wa-
tered so much he could not see to sew, and he
got laryngitis and lost his voice.

So now he couldn't hoot worth a darn or darn
worth a hoot!

There was a young lady from Orange
Who insisted on coming from Orange;
    She troubled my mind
    Since I never could find
A suitable rhyme for Orange.

FAMOUS FLY

Once upon a time there was a fly who really put himself on the map. He got squashed in an atlas.

———•———

I've just heard a terrible rumor
  Which I'm hoping is not true at all:
That the best-looking girl at a prizefight
  Is known as the belle of the brawl.

———•———

Q. What's a bow tie?
A. Two winners in an archery contest.

———•———

Sound Barrier

Ancient Egypt, in days of King Tut,
Had goddesses named Nut and Mut;
Now, Nut was "Noot" and Mut was "Moot"
And Tut was rightly pronounced as "Toot."
But with names like that, I'm forced to say,
They'd hardly make the grade today;
To vote for Tut and worship Mut
You'd have to be some kind of Nut,
And as for Toot and Noot and Moot—
      They're a hoot!

———•———

FEARSOME
FRANK

Here lies the body of Fearsome Frank,
Who often bet he could rob any bank,
And bragged he had never lost a bet
        Yet.

———————•———————

Knock! knock!
Who's there?
Yule.
Yule who?
Yule see!

NEPTUNE'S REVENGE
A Tale of the Sea

Three men were fishing in the Gulf of Mexico when one of them pulled in a huge fish.

But as soon as it was in the boat the fish shook the hook out of its mouth and changed into an angry bearded man wearing a crown and brandishing a three-pronged spear.

"Who are you, sir?" quavered one of the fishermen.

"I am Neptune, god of the sea, and I am going to put a curse on you! Before you get home, your boat will spring a dozen leaks—nay, make that a dozen and a half, just for good measure!"

With a nasty laugh Neptune dived over the side and disappeared. The fishermen's boat got so many holes in it that they had to swim ashore, and from that day to this they have never forgotten Neptune's eighteen-hole Gulf curse.

Our hostess at a party was passing around appetizers.

"I hope you're not on one of your silly diets, Stanley," she said.

Stanley Winters gave the appetizers a stern look.

"I never eat fish on Sunday. However, since today is not Sunday and these aren't fish, I'll make an exception," he said, and took one.

BARNABUS BAKER

Here lies the body of Barnabus Baker,
Prominent local undertaker;
He's lying here now, one might say,
Taking a busman's holiday.

———●———

FAMOUS CRIMES OF HISTORY

Two young pages at the court of Transylvania always carried the end of the queen's robe, which was covered with priceless gems, in royal processions.

One day they tore it loose and ran away with it. This was known, of course, as the Great Train Robbery.

———●———

Did I ever tell you I write headlines for a newspaper run by trained animals? The gnus are in charge of the headline department, and they pay very well. You'd be surprised how much the newspaper headline gnus pay per headline!*

You mean this is supposed to be funny??

Knock! knock!
Who's there?
Serge.
Serge who?
Serge me!

"BEEFEATER"
BERRIEN

Here lies the body of "Beefeater" Berrien;
He should have been a vegetarian.

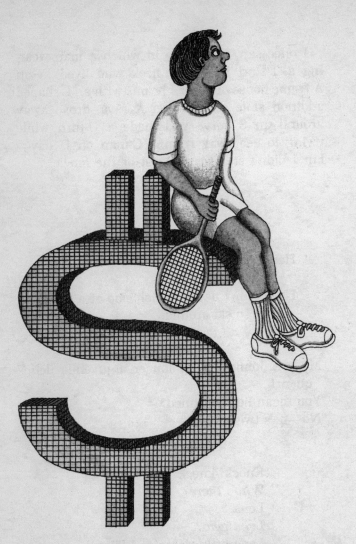

Q. What do tennis pros make?
A. Net profit.

I once saw a B movie in which a man wearing a T-shirt with a V neck who lived in an A-frame house made of I beams with an L-shaped addition stole some secret X rays, drove away around an S curve and made a U-turn while trying to get away from a G-man on D day—but I didn't stay for the rest of the movie.

LESTER LEE

Here lies the body of Lester Lee
　　　　Underground;
He couldn't decide which side of a tree
　　　　To ski around.

"My son Johnny is no longer a juvenile delinquent!"
"You mean he's reformed?"
"No—he's twenty-one!"

Knock! knock!
Who's there?
Lena.
Lena who?
Lena little closer and I'll tell you.

OSCAR
ORM

Here lies the body of Oscar Orm,
Whose notion of practical jokes was odd;
Snuck out in the midst of a thunderstorm
And tried to steal a lightning rod.

NEW BOOKS

The Vanishing Chinaman
by Heidi Quickee

The Spanish Aviator
by Lupe de Loop

**SAMUEL
SMITH**

Here lies the body of Samuel Smith;
What was that stuff he was fooling with?

———————•———————

"What's that cute drum majorette's hotel room
    number?"
"Suite 16."

———————•———————

State Secrets

A driver in Tenn.'s Chattanooga
Has a horn that still makes an *ah-oo-gah!*
    For he's driving a car
    That is older by far
Than most of downtown Chattanooga.

A tenor from Idaho's Boise
Has a voice no one out there enjoys; he
    Can practice all day
    And be heard miles away;
He's a whole lot too noisy for Boise.

Q. What does an orchestra need when it wants to play the "Minute" Waltz in two seconds?
A. A lightning conductor.

"Look, Tonto! On faraway hill, Navahos send up smoke signal. What does smoke signal say?"
"Smoke signal say No Smoking on Reservation."

Q. How did the mountain climber feel when he tumbled off the top of the mountain?
A. Crestfallen.

Math Problem

John takes a drive from A to C by way of B. John drives 40 miles per hour. The distances are 120 miles from A to B and 60 miles from B to C.

1. How long does it take John to drive from A to C by way of B?
2. How long would it take John to drive directly from A to C?

Answers

1. Well, according to John, he looked at his watch when he left A, and it was 9:30 on the dot. But when he looked again later on, his watch had stopped. However, when he reached B, he noticed the clock on the town hall said 12:30, so it must have taken him about 3 hours plus whatever time it took him to get from B to C.
2. You can't drive straight from A to C because the bridge is out.

When some folks go to bed
   They start counting sheep.
I never got the hang of it.
   I always fall asleep.

Knock! knock!
Who's there?
Hoodoo.
Hoodoo who?
Hoodoo you think?

Q. What's television in a tent?
A. TPTV.

It all depends on your point of view;
This much I can confirm:
A hole in an apple is bad news to you
But it's home, sweet home to a worm.

State Secrets

A girl from Ol' Miss's Biloxi
Once proved Southern belles can be foxy;
 When a Yankee upstart
 Claimed she'd broken his heart
She mended the thing with epoxy!

A girl from Rhode Island's Pawtucket
Found a ring in an old oaken bucket;
 Her father she told;
 He saw it was gold,
And the first thing she knew, her Paw tucket!

NEW BOOKS

Saddle Sores
by Rhoda Bronco

Heaven Forbid!
by Shirley Nott

Hidden Woes
by Sigrid Sorrow

"What's on the menu today?"
"Everything from A to Z!"
But only one dish was on the menu. What
 was it?*

KATE
McFEE

Here lies the body of Kate McFee,
Who died at the age of a hundred and three;
Tried everything new; never was *Kate* bored;
Still, she shouldn't have tried a skateboard.

Knock! knock!
Who's there?
Alaska who?
Alaska question now. Knock! knock!
Who's there?
Hawaii.
Fine, thanks. Who else is there?
Iowa.
Iowa who?
Iowa buck to Ohio.
Ohio who?
Ohio Malley, and how's Mrs. O'Malley?

BREWSTER B.
BRECKENRIDGE

Here lies the body of Brewster B.;
Since I shot him he ain't what he uster be.

Never Seen Again

A famous explorer
   Was Roderick Mungle;
He could find his way
   Through any jungle;
But he soon disappeared
   While visiting Boston;
I often have wondered
   What street he got lost on.

Here lies the body of Winifred Wexpert,
Wrongly self-styled mushroom expert.

Q. What happened to the explorer who met a cannibal tribe for the first time?
A. He was consumed with curiosity.

———•———

There once was a girl from East Lynn—
Or was it West Lynn she was in?
    I knew which, and yet
    Right now I forget . . .
Some days you just can't win!

———•———

Q. What do Chinese sailors eat?
A. Junk food.

———•———

BERTRAM
BUNCE

Here lies the body of Bertram Bunce,
Whose brain had long begun to soften;
He was always ready to try anything once
    Too often.

———•———

IT SUITS ME FINE

I guess we all know what nudists wear to birthday parties, don't we?

———•———

Dracula and I were boyhood friends. I knew
him when he was just a little nipper.

———————•———————

Q. What's a box lunch?
A. A square meal.

———————•———————

Q. What's a lunch counter?
A. The person at the cash register.

———————•———————

"I'll give you a piece of my mind!"
"Okay, I'll lend you my tweezers."

———————•———————

NEW BOOKS

De Hole in De Ship
by Mandy Pumps

A New Slant on Life
by Eileen Sideways

The Flaming IOU
by Bernadette

"What are you doing?"
"I'm having twenty winks."
"You mean, forty winks, don't you?"
"No, I'm only half-asleep."

Double Exposure

Two pairs of Siamese twins
    Showed up one night at our place.
It was fascinating to see them meet
    Face to face to face to face.

"The Smiths are moving to a better neighborhood."
"It won't be when they get there."

ANCIENT SAYING

Scout who pitches pup tent wrong way
ends up in doghouse.

———•———

Q. What do we have when there's no snow?
A. Tough sledding.

———•———

HAYS
McVALE

Here lies the body of Hays McVale,
A butcher who died with his thumb on the scale;
A customer shot him, thus causing Hays
To regret the errors of his weighs.

———•———

NEW BOOKS

Put Kids to Work!
by Hiram Young

The Heavy Burden
by Aiken Back

The Tiresome Talker
by Boris Stiff

The Sunbather
by Baird Hyde

———•———

The latest Broadway musical takes place in a steam bath. It's called *The Sauna Music*.

King Henry the Eighth was a famous glutton.
You wouldn't believe how much Henry VIII!

What Aols Them?

By all that's sacred! By the Holy Grail!
Why do the English spell *jail* as *gaol*?
Who would want to travel by raol,
Or shop in a store at a Clearance Saol,
Or ride to hounds over hill and daol?
Why do the English spell *jail* as *gaol*?

———————•———————

First Ant: Run! Here comes an anteater!
Second Ant: Stop kidding! I don't see any an——

———————•———————

DARCY
BUELL

Here lies the body of Darcy Buell,
The second-best shot in a famous duel.

———————•———————

WRONG AGAIN

One day Joey found his friend Herbie down on his knees beside a large hole in the ground.

"What are you doing *now*, Herbie?" sighed Joey.

"There's a talking fox in this hole," said Herbie. "I know he's in there, and I want him to come out and talk to me."

"Don't be silly, Herbie, there's no talking fox in that hole."

Just then a fox trotted around the side of a nearby rock.

"Your friend's right, Herbie," said the fox. "I've been out here hiding behind this rock the whole time."

"You see, Herbie?" said Joey. "I *told* you there wasn't any talking fox in that hole!"

———————•———————

Q. What are good manners called in Warsaw?
A. Polish polish.

Heavenly Daze!

When someone tries to tempt you
Into doing something wrong,
Temptation put behind you!
Be noble! good! and strong!
Recall this old-time rule;
Remember how it goes:
Evil whispers yes,
Goodness only noes!

OLD JOKES NEVER DIE

A terrible three-piece orchestra in a big restaurant was playing "My Old Kentucky Home" when the violinist noticed that a guest at a nearby table was weeping bitterly.

"Pardon me, sir," asked the violinist, "are you a Kentuckian?"

"No," sobbed the guest, "I'm a musician!"

Q. Why did the elephant stand sideways on his head?
A. He wanted to keep a low profile.

OLD JOKES NEVER DIE

"I've been poisoned!" cried Big Bad Bill, and fell into a stupor. Someone was always leaving the lid off the stupor.

———————•———————

Q. What's a blunderbuss?
A. A school bus on the wrong road.

———————•———————

Q. What did the elephant do when he came to the water hole?
A. He sliced his drive into the woods.

———————•———————

Q. Why does an elephant rub vanishing cream on his body?
A. It helps an elephant hide.

———————•———————

"Instead of eating at home last night we had dinner in a famous French restaurant, and oh! what a difference!"

"What *was* the difference?"

"About seventy dollars."

MORTIMER
GISSING

Here lies the body of Mortimer Gissing;
His famous last words: "I hear something hissing!"

THE MUSICIAN'S REVENGE

Persnikoff, the world's second-greatest violinist, was madly jealous of Morgenstern, the world's greatest violinist. Persnikoff decided to make himself the greatest.

He worked out a devilishly ingenious mechanism that would be triggered by only one sound —the sound of a G the way Morgenstern played it on his violin.

Next he made a bomb for the devilishly ingenious mechanism to set off.

Next he put in his pocket a key to Morgenstern's apartment, which he had stolen earlier so that he could sneak in and hide the bomb before Morgenstern came home.

Before leaving his own apartment he did one more thing. Just to make sure Morgenstern was not home (Persnikoff knew he had a rehearsal scheduled for that morning with the world's greatest symphony orchestra), Persnikoff decided to telephone Morgenstern's apartment.

When the police questioned Morgenstern about the explosion in Persnikoff's apartment, all he could say was,

"Well, my rehearsal was called off, so I was home practicing. The phone rang and I said to my wife, 'get the phone, will you?' She heard Persnikoff's voice. Meanwhile, I kept right on playing Mozart's Concerto in G Major—and suddenly my wife heard a terrible explosion! . . ."

The Wrong Hold

The sexton, who cared for the church,
    Taught his son how to ring the bell.
Said he, "On some sad occasions
    You will have to toll the knell.
If you want to do things right
    And know you have properly tolled it,
You must learn the bell-rope holds,
    For it's all in the way you hold it.
Now, whenever you toll the knell,
    That means someone's life is done,
But if you stop in the middle,
    That's only a half-knell, son."

Q. Which king did the elephants fear the most?
A. Richard the Mouse-Hearted.

Once upon a time there was a worm who worked in a compost pile. He was very ambitious and wanted to get to the top of the heap, so one morning he started work half an hour early.

But when he did, all the grubs and beetles jeered at him and made rude noises, which only goes to prove the old adage, The Early Worm Gets The Bird.

Knock! knock!
Who's there?
Dwayne.
Dwayne who?
Dwayne is leaking through dwoof!

Knock! knock!
Who's there?
Heidi.
Heidi who?
Heidi ho!

An astronomer up in Poughkeepsie
Once picked the wrong day to be tipsy;
    When the moon hid the sun
    He missed all the fun,
And never did he the eclipse see!

My little sister is so dumb
she thinks a southpaw is a Southern daddy.

There once was a monster named Hyde
Who sneered in a manner quite snide,
    "Just think what a wreck'll
    Become of Doc Jekyll
When he finds out he's got *me* inside!"

HERE LIES
THE BODY
OF
JEFFREY
SQUATTUM
~o~o~o~o
IN SKIN-DIVING
CLASS HE CAME
OUT AT THE
BOTTOM

---•---

It is estimated that the average man spends over two thousand hours during his lifetime combing his hair. That's why bald men get so much more done.

---•---

The Oyster's Lament

That anyone can eat us
   To us oysters seems incredible;
We do everything we can to make
   Ourselves appear inedible!

---•---

SIMEON
SHEDD

Here lies the body of Simeon Shedd;
Told me where to go; I sent him on ahead.

---•---

The lowest form of wit
Is a nit.

---•---

GREGORY
GENTIAN

Here lies the body of Gregory Gentian;
What happened to him's too awful to mention.

---•---

A Great Career Cut Short

Merry Andrew won great renown
As the Middle Ages' most famous clown.
Andrew laughed at everything.
One day he laughed at a grouchy king.
Since then, whenever his name is read off,
He's recalled as the man who laughed his head off.

DOUBLE BUNK

"Why don't you take the top bunk for a change?"
"No, I don't want to oversleep."

Why Poets Go Crazy

Fingers
Rhymes with lingers
But doesn't rhyme with singers;
They look as if they should;
I only wish they would!
But though singers
Rhymes with ringers
And with wingers
And humdingers,
None of 'em rhyme with fingers,
Which only rhymes with lingers
(And, you may have noticed, lingers
Only rhymes with fingers!)*

---

* *If you don't believe this, read it aloud.*

I should have known better than to ask Stanley Winters where he was going.

"I'm going to buy a vacuum cleaner," he said. "There's nothing I hate worse than a dirty vacuum!"

Q. What happened to the poet who got up in the morning and wrote a poem?

A. He went from bed to verse.

Q. How can you make an elephant laugh?
A. Tell him a rhinoceros joke.

HOW SASKATCHEWAN GOT ITS NAME

In the early days in Canada one man owned most of the land in what later became the province of Saskatchewan. One day he was riding around on his property when he found a trespasser camped there.

When he told the fellow to get off his land, the trespasser gave him a lot of lip, whereupon the owner yelled, "Don't give me none of your sass! Katchewan my property again and I'll have the law on ye!"

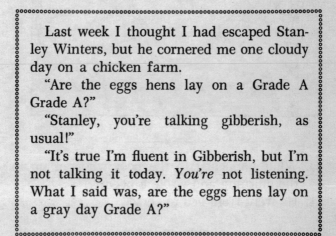

Last week I thought I had escaped Stanley Winters, but he cornered me one cloudy day on a chicken farm.

"Are the eggs hens lay on a Grade A Grade A?"

"Stanley, you're talking gibberish, as usual!"

"It's true I'm fluent in Gibberish, but I'm not talking it today. *You're* not listening. What I said was, are the eggs hens lay on a gray day Grade A?"

Knock! knock!
Who's there?
Thatcher.
Thatcher who?
Thatcher idea of a joke?

Q. Why did the taxidermist overeat?
A. He was trying to stuff himself.

Q. How can you tell how much a tapeworm eats?
A. Buy him a tape recorder.

My uncle was an ornithologist who wrote a terrible bird guide. He was a bird-watcher and a word-botcher.

Q. What happened when the cannibals captured the skinny missionary?

A. They had slim pickings.

Here *should* lie the body of Spooky Green;
Last seen
On Halloween.

I know a photographer who specializes in portraits of infants. He's always looking for baby sitters.

EDGAR FINCH'S DOOM
A Tale of the Occult

One dark and dismal night a young man named Edgar Finch was passing a fortune-teller's parlor when he felt a sudden strange and irresistible impulse to go inside and have his fortune told.

Seated at a table in a dimly lit room was a withered old crone in a Gypsy costume. She asked Edgar a few questions in a low, hoarse voice, then leaned forward and peered deeply into the large crystal ball that stood on the table before her.

She scarcely looked into the crystal ball when she fell back in her chair with a shriek.

"Death! I see Death!" she wailed. "Go! I must tell you no more! Go! go!" she cried, and Edgar Finch turned and rushed into the night filled with a sense of impending doom.

Edgar is eighty-five now, but to this day he has never quite got rid of that sense of impending doom.

OLD JOKES NEVER DIE

It's no wonder George Washington was able to throw a dollar across the Rappahannock River. A dollar went farther in those days.

---◆---

BOOK LIST

The Return of the Sprinter
by Ransom More

Demolition Derby
by Rex Carrs

Stop Fidgeting!
by Stan Still

Petty Thief
by Robin Piggybank

This is the End
by Saul Over

Raindrops Fallin' on My Head
by Rufus Leakin

---◆---

Q. When the soprano missed a high note at the ship's concert, how did the audience feel?
A. C-sick.

---◆---

"I hear that fat teacher threw you out of class. What happened?"

"Nothing much. She read us a poem about courage, and then she said, 'My motto is Keep Your Chin Up!,' and I said, 'Which one?'"

---◆---

---•---

Everything is getting too modern. Last Halloween I saw a witch riding a vacuum cleaner.

---•---

JOHNNY DOW

Here lies the body of Johnny Dow;
A liar once, a lier now.

---•---

Anatomy Lesson

Each part of our body, it's easy to show,
Has its own special job, from our brains to our heart,
But what about our middle toe?
What is its function, what is its art?
Well, it's very important, I'll have you know:
It keeps our other toes apart.

---•---

PAIR PERISH IN DUEL

HAROLD HUFF	HUBERT HEARST
Here lies the body Of Harold Huff; Harold fired first, But not first enough.	Here lies the body Of Hubert Hearst; Hubert fired second, But near enough first.

---•---

A dashing young man from Decatur
Tried to dash up a Down escalator;
    Can you blame the poor dude?
    He was being pursued
By a twenty-four-foot alligator!

You may ask how a huge alligator
Ever strayed all the way to Decatur;
    You may ask, as I say;
    You certainly may;
But please don't ask now—escalator!

———•———

    Knock! knock!
    Who's there?
    Chester.
    Chester who?
    Chester man you're looking for!

———•———

One morning on a bird walk I found Stanley Winters snapping a scarlet tanager.

"What kind of film are you using, Stanley?"

"Black and white."

"What? You're taking that beautiful bird in black and white? Don't you ever use color film for birds?"

"Only penguins."

Short Story

Once upon a time, five seconds ago,
I started this poem with a capital O.
In another five seconds, as you will see,
I am going to end it with a capital Z.

Q. Why did the elephant guard the haystack?
A. He was watching his diet.

MUSCLES DUCHARME

Here lies the body of Muscles Ducharme,
Champion weight lifter. Came to harm
When somebody tickled him under the arm.

ADVICE TO SARCASTIC SMALL BOYS

Don't tend to belittle if you tend to be little.

A rich and famous
Model is Kitty.
How does she do it?
She's sitting pretty.

THE TORTOISE AND THE HARE

One day a tortoise woke up, stuck his head out of his shell, and found a hare staring at him. The tortoise became very angry.

"No, you don't!" he cried. "If you think you're going to get *me* into one of those silly fables that end with a MORAL you've got another think coming!" he said, and pulled his head back into his shell.

Moral: Not everybody likes morals.

Q. Name three famous Poles.
A. North, South, and Tad.

The other day I made the mistake of saying something to Stanley Winters about a state dinner, which is a very formal dinner with lots of bigwigs present.

"I went to a state dinner once," said Stanley. "We had Kentucky fried chicken, Virginia ham, Idaho potatoes, Georgia peaches, New York steak, and baked Alaska with Hawaiian pineapple."

"Wait a minute, what's New York steak?"

"Oh, that was very unusual. It was Buffalo meat!"

A sourpuss
    Was Auntie May.
Her welcome mat
    Said Stay Away!

———•———

Sights to See

The Roman Forum's a place to go roamin' for 'em,
And Peru's emphatically a place to peruse 'em;
There's very good peeking one can do in Peking,
And the Pyramids are nice to peer amid.

———•———

NEW BOOKS

The Star Spangled Banner
by José Cañusi

Baker's Man
by Pat E. Cake

The Fatal Curse
by Mayhew Dropdead

"I once had a high school principal whose principal failing was that he had no principles where my principal was concerned," said Stanley Winters. "One time he borrowed money from me and never paid it back."

"What did you do about it?"

"Nothing. I lost interest. I also lost the money, but I still had the principal. He taught me a lesson!"

Knock! knock!
Who's there?
Knock.
Knock who?
Knock it off, we've had enough!

———•———

SCOTT CORBETT is a serious joke-collector. He earned his first writing credits for one-liners in magazines like *The Saturday Evening Post,* and wrote jokes for radio and for *Yank,* the army weekly during World War II.

A novelist and former English teacher, he is the author of funny books like *The Limerick Trick* and *The Discontented Ghost.* He is a humorist, collector of ghost stories, and world traveler who lives in Providence, Rhode Island.

ANNIE GUSMAN has illustrated several funny books for kids—*Rat Stew* is one—and for adults. She studied drawing in Boston, Greece, and Rhode Island, and now lives in Brookline, Massachusetts.